Are You Over the Hill?

Find Out Before It's Too Late!

By Bill Dodds

Illustrated by Stephen Carpenter

Meadowbrook Press
Distributed by Simon & Schuster
New York

Library of Congress Cataloging-in-Publication Data

Dodds, Bill.
    Are you over the hill? : find out before it's too late!
    / by Bill Dodds ; illustrated by Stephen Carpenter.
        p.   cm.
    1.   Middle age—Humor.   I.   Title
    PN6231.M47D59 1993
    818'.5402—dc20   93-40832
                                                               CIP
ISBN: 0-88166-207-0
Simon & Schuster Ordering #: 0-671-88445-X

Published by Meadowbrook Press, 18318 Minnetonka Boulevard, Deephaven, Minnesota 55391.

BOOK TRADE DISTRIBUTION by Simon & Schuster, a division of Simon and Schuster, Inc., 1230 Avenue of the Americas, New York, NY 10020.

Managing Editor: Dale E. Howard
Editorial Coordinator: Cathy Broberg
Production Manager: Amy Unger
Desktop Publishing Manager: Jon C. Wright
Illustrator: Stephen Carpenter

Copyright © 1994 by Bill Dodds

99 98 97 96 95 94   6 5 4 3 2

Printed in the United States of America

Contents

Dedication

For Monica, whom I love so much I'm not even going to mention that she is three months, two weeks, and two days older than I am (not counting daylight saving time).

Introduction

Just Inches Past the Peak

Are congratulations in order? Is this the year you reached new personal and professional heights? As you stand tall and look around, do you realize you have nowhere to go but down?

You—over the hill? Impossible!

All your friends, family, and co-workers must be wrong. Sure, that's it. And you can prove it. Just put on those new reading glasses, take a few minutes, and browse through *Are You Over the Hill?*.

It's not describing you. Not at all.

Well, not all the time. Okay, maybe sometimes.

Okay, maybe more often now than even a few years ago, but still. . . .

Okay, technically you may be over the hill, but really you're just inches past the peak.

Heading down.

Gaining speed.

You need to have the hair in your ears trimmed.

Let's Get Physical

You've tried every weight-loss program ever invented and have even created a few of your own.

❖

You call them "laugh lines," not "crow's-feet" or "wrinkles."

❖

You have a wart older than the paperboy.

❖

You're beginning to see the long-term effects of gravity on certain body parts.

You wonder how you'll look with false teeth.

❖

You can't sleep on a soft mattress without getting a backache.

❖

You don't mind wearing bifocals because it's just so nice to be able to see print clearly again.

❖

You eat less red meat.

❖

You accidentally snort when you laugh hard.

❖

You haven't changed the color of your hair or lipstick in five years.

❖

When you hear the phrase "hot flash," you don't think "news bulletin."

The kid bagging your groceries just assumes you'll want help carrying them to the car.

❖

You don't drink anything with caffeine after 5 P.M.

❖

You don't eat cookie dough because it has raw eggs in it.

❖

Your knees pop when you walk.

❖

Your ankles swell on a regular basis.

❖

You avoid looking in full-length mirrors.

❖

You only read in a room that's well lit.

You need to have the hair in your ears trimmed.

❖

You don't bother counting or pulling your gray hairs anymore.

❖

You don't go anywhere without a toothpick in your purse or pocket.

❖

You don't wear spandex.

❖

You like shopping for shoes because that's your one size that never changes.

❖

You let out an involuntary grunt when you get up from the sofa.

❖

You consider cellulite an old friend.

You haven't had a pimple in a quarter of a century.

❖

You're convinced more people are mumbling these days.

❖

You can comb your hair with a towel.

❖

Your butt has disappeared.

❖

Your butt is growing at an alarming rate.

❖

You're sure today's size twelve is the same as size eight was twenty years ago.

❖

You can't see the numbers on the bathroom scale without sucking in your stomach.

You refer to gray hair as "silver."

❖

You check your hands for liver spots.

❖

You have a "crack" problem—especially when you bend over (and the back of your pants slides down even farther).

❖

You have to buckle your belt below your waistline.

❖

You're positive that you used to be taller.

❖

You can't sleep on the other side of the bed.

❖

You have a "touch" of arthritis that lets you know when the weather is about to change.

You think there's nothing quite like a good
bowel movement.

❖

The skin under your biceps flaps in the breeze.

❖

Tiny veins are appearing on your nose.

❖

You regret getting that tattoo.

❖

You need to rock forward and backward
a couple of times to propel yourself out of a low,
soft easy-chair.

❖

You have a newfound sympathy for your aunt
who used to go on and on about her bursitis.

❖

You hope being young at heart makes up for
being middle-aged in a lot of other places.

You prefer wearing a silly hat to having a cold head.

On the Road

You always go to the bathroom before you head out.

❖

You wouldn't think of leaving the house without a tissue or hankie in your pocket.

❖

You prefer wearing a silly hat to having a cold head.

❖

You never drive over 55 mph anymore.

❖

The last time you exceeded the speed limit, the officer who pulled you over looked like a kid playing cop.

To get into the car, you sit down first and then swing both legs in.

❖

You travel with an inflatable, doughnut-shaped seat cushion.

❖

You constantly ask for directions.

❖

You always carry a map.

❖

You stop for gas when there's a quarter of a tank left.

❖

You drive for miles without noticing that your left turn signal is on.

❖

You listen to radio stations that feature all-news or golden oldies.

You often quote National Public Radio's
"All Things Considered."

❖

You don't even bother trying to parallel park.

❖

You wander the mall parking lot, searching for your car.

❖

You don't even consider changing a flat tire but
immediately call AAA.

❖

You can't wait until you qualify for senior-citizen discounts.

❖

Your idea of roughing it is a motel without cable TV.

❖

You have trouble falling asleep in a motel because you
miss your own pillow.

Your pet's cremated remains are in an urn on the mantel.

Family Life

You dream about the things you're going to do once your youngest child moves out.

❖

You've noticed that your younger siblings look middle-aged.

❖

You hear your kids using some of your favorite sayings on *their* kids.

❖

Your youngest child is older than you were when you had your oldest child.

You trust your children's driving.

❖

All of your children have moved out—and back again.

❖

You get nervous when your parents and kids start whispering to each other.

❖

Your parents are *really* old.

❖

You've called a cease-fire with your mother-in-law.

❖

You and your spouse are relying more and more on mental telepathy—and it's working.

❖

You talk to your pet more often than you talk to anyone else in the house.

Your pet is more understanding than anyone else
in the house.

❖

You hang up a Christmas stocking for your pet and don't
care what anyone thinks about it.

❖

Your pet's cremated remains are in an urn on the mantel.

❖

You spring new recipes on your family whether they'll like
them or not, because they look good to you.

❖

At family reunions, you have a guaranteed spot at
the "big" table.

❖

You're beginning to look more like your mother or father.

You fall asleep in front of the TV but pop awake and complain, "I was watching that," when your spouse tiptoes by and turns it off.

❖

Your kids are concerned about your spending habits because they think of your savings as their inheritance.

❖

You realize any couple can end up divorced.

❖

You understand why your mother always wore a sweater.

❖

You know that spoiling your grandchildren is the best revenge.

❖

You know you haven't actually mellowed; you're just always tired.

You think about the specific diseases your ancestors had.

❖

Your younger siblings don't hesitate to mention that they are your *younger* siblings.

❖

You're sure that kids today whine more than they talk.

❖

You still offer sound advice to your children, even though you know they don't listen to you any more than you listened to your parents.

❖

You've stopped borrowing money from your parents.

❖

A few toddlers are running around calling you "Grandma" or "Grandpa."

You really don't care what the neighbors think.

Older but Wiser

You know how many times Liz Taylor has been married.

❖

You can admit to yourself that you're never going to own
waterfront property.

❖

You get along with your ex-husband.

❖

You get along with your ex-wife.

❖

You often tell yourself, "You're as young as you feel." The
problem is, most of the time you don't feel young.

You hang up all your clothes without someone
asking you to.

❖

You vacuum and straighten up the living room even
when people aren't coming over.

❖

You find yourself praying a lot.

❖

You've learned it's easier to forgive.

❖

You hurt when you see others hurting.

❖

You wonder what this country's coming to.

❖

You know that money isn't everything—it won't buy
happiness, and you certainly can't take it with you.

You pick your fights more carefully and win more often.

❖

You know the strong don't always survive, while the flexible usually do.

❖

You really don't care what the neighbors think.

❖

You never go to a restaurant without making a reservation first.

❖

You always read the directions first.

❖

You don't sweat the small stuff.

❖

You lift with your legs, not your back.

You balance your checkbook every month when
the statement comes.

❖

You look before you leap and often decide not to leap.

❖

You know the value of a dollar (about twenty-five cents).

❖

You care less about style and more about comfort.

❖

You know Nixon used to be a vice president.

❖

You put on your glasses and read the fine print
before signing something.

❖

You know you're never going to learn to play the piano.

You're no longer surprised when someone does something surprising.

❖

You make sure there's toilet paper on the roll before you sit down.

❖

You don't like the thought of growing old but prefer it to the only alternative.

❖

You're pleased by how much you know about people now, compared to what you knew twenty-five years ago.

❖

You know life doesn't end at forty.

You wear underwear under your pajamas.

Sex

You didn't turn to this chapter first, even though it was clearly marked "Sex."

❖

You turned to this chapter as soon as you were sure no one was watching.

❖

You emphasize quality, not quantity.

❖

At the county fair, you prefer the food concession stand to the tunnel of love.

You don't even bother sucking in your stomach or thrusting out your chest when an attractive young member of the opposite sex walks by.

❖

You suck in your stomach or thrust out your chest when an attractive, slightly older member of the opposite sex walks by.

❖

On a cold winter's night, your thoughts turn to your electric blanket.

❖

You wear underwear under your pajamas.

❖

Afterward, you get up and put your pajamas back on.

❖

You're too embarrassed to watch an R-rated movie with your kids or your parents.

You could write a book on sex—or at least a chapter.

❖

Sometimes you think it's nice just to snuggle.

❖

You think a touch, smile, glance, or sigh shared with someone special can say it all.

❖

You can't get used to seeing condoms right next to the Pepto-Bismol at the grocery store.

❖

You know that Sleeping Beauty probably drooled on her pillow and that Prince Charming must have smelled like his big white horse.

❖

The only reason you're ever up at 3 A.M. is because you have to use the bathroom.

❖

You have a lot of fond memories about sex.

You've got your own filing system, and it works as long as
no one touches *anything* on your desk.

On the Job

....

You've been promoted to the point that you don't know what you're doing, but you know a lot more than anyone else.

❖

You have eight months' worth of sick leave stored up.

❖

You can't get the hang of transferring a call on the new telephone system.

❖

You've got your own filing system, and it works as long as no one touches *anything* on your desk.

❖

You still marvel at what computers can do.

Your boss is just a kid.

❖

You're the only one at the office who remembers what a typewriter bell sounds like and which side of the carbon paper faces up.

❖

You don't read or write memos.

❖

You remember when it took only twenty minutes to get to work.

❖

You arrive a little early and don't leave until the work day is over.

❖

You would rather be busy than just try to look busy.

❖

You notice that the weeks go by fast, but payday doesn't come often enough.

You feel guilty for running something off on the copy machine for your personal use.

❖

You still can't figure out how to use the fax machine.

❖

You rinse out your coffee mug before green stuff starts growing in the bottom of it.

❖

You know that there are no peaceful times at work, only different kinds of crises.

❖

You figure they can't fire you because you know where all the bodies are buried (you've helped dig a few of the graves).

❖

You keep your own stash of aspirin and antacids.

❖

You haven't stolen any office supplies in years.

You've given up any hope of winning the football pool.

❖

You don't bother taking notes at staff meetings anymore (you've heard it all before).

❖

You keep your mouth shut, even though you know a proposed idea has been tried before and didn't work.

❖

You stay sober at the Christmas party.

❖

You've discovered there's something to be said for loyalty.

❖

You've analyzed the advantages and disadvantages of a monthly retirement check versus a lump-sum payment.

❖

You've opened an IRA.

You spend time daydreaming at work about the unforgettable speech you're going to make at your retirement party.

❖

You know you don't have to be retired to join AARP.

❖

You know what AARP stands for.

❖

You know at what age Social Security kicks in.

❖

You wonder how much you're *really* going to get back from Social Security.

❖

You're making more than you ever dreamed, and it's buying less than you ever imagined.

You love a good nap.

Likes and Dislikes

You no longer like the Beatles' song "When I'm Sixty-Four."

❖

You don't like it when someone refers to fifty years as "half a century."

❖

You're starting to resent that the period in Western history marked by bubonic plague, ignorance, and early death is known as the "Middle Ages."

❖

You consider brown sugar on your oatmeal a real treat.

You like hearing stories about people who are still active in their eighties and nineties.

❖

You like vegetables that used to make you gag.

❖

You don't like paperback books with small type.

❖

You love a good nap.

❖

You think the people who complain about turning forty are a bunch of whiners.

❖

You don't like the songs teenagers are listening to today because you can't understand the lyrics.

❖

You sing along with Karen Carpenter songs.

You don't like leaving messages on answering machines.

❖

You don't like the sound of your voice on tape.

❖

You're beginning to find polyester more appealing.

❖

You no longer laugh at guys wearing white shoes or white belts.

❖

You hate it when someone hangs a new roll of toilet paper in the "wrong" direction.

❖

It bothers you that certain presidents were your age or younger when they were in office.

❖

You're beginning to like the "Family Circus" comic strip more than you used to and are afraid to admit that you just don't get "The Far Side."

You have to loosen your belt buckle to watch
TV after dinner.

Now That's Entertainment

You think PG-13 movies are just a little too racy.

❖

You spend more time in the Classics section of the video store than in New Releases.

❖

When you can't find a classic to rent, you settle for a Disney movie.

❖

You wouldn't dream of returning a videotape without rewinding it first.

❖

You can't figure out how to program your VCR—you have to get your grandchildren to do it for you.

You hate "colorized" movies.

❖

Your favorite actor's granddaughter is now starring in
an R-rated movie.

❖

When you hear the term "CD," you think "certificate of
deposit," not "compact disc."

❖

You no longer turn up the bass all the way.

❖

You can't name a single Top 40 song.

❖

You have to loosen your belt buckle to watch
TV after dinner.

❖

You can't believe that the people in denture-adhesive
commercials are so young.

You can't name the hosts of the late-night talk shows because you can't stay awake that long anymore.

❖

The last time you watched "Saturday Night Live," you kept asking "Who's that?" and didn't laugh once.

❖

The actor who played the little kid on your favorite soap opera is now a grandparent.

❖

You prefer PBS to the network stations.

❖

You laugh uproariously at the Three Stooges.

❖

You'd rather watch an entire show you can't stand than get up and change the channel.

❖

You scan the obituaries before reading the comics.

You find it hard not to laugh at the hairdos teenagers are sporting these days.

In My Opinion

You can't believe how conservative you've become and how liberal your parents seem to be these days.

❖

You don't hesitate to answer, "Yes, I *do* mind if you smoke."

❖

You know there will never be another Hitchcock.

❖

You no longer cringe when a younger person calls you "Sir" or "Madam."

❖

You think proper foot care is important.

You wonder when TV got so stupid.

❖

You prefer Marilyn to Madonna.

❖

You've noticed lately that old people really aren't that old,
but young people seem *awfully* young.

❖

You're sure you're a lot younger than people your age
used to be.

❖

You think phone calls should cost a dime.

❖

You think getting up as late as a quarter to nine in the
morning is sleeping in.

❖

Your idea of living on the edge is trying a new brand
of deodorant.

You find it hard not to laugh at the hairdos teenagers are sporting these days.

❖

You pretend to listen sincerely when some twenty-year-old tells you how all the world's problems can be solved.

❖

You now realize your father was right: the world *is* going to hell in a hand basket.

❖

You hate rap music.

❖

You've noticed that there are no longer any good presidential candidates.

❖

You're happy to share your opinion anywhere, anytime—except, of course, for a telephone survey.

❖

You agree—Muhammad Ali *was* the greatest.

You can't remember the last time you did the limbo.

Thanks for the Memories

When you hear the name "Fonda," you think Henry, or even Jane, but *never* Bridget.

❖

When you were a kid, you could eat your Halloween candy without inspecting it for pins.

❖

You know what "sputnik" was.

❖

You think the Dodgers belong in Brooklyn.

❖

You grew up before the days of "Sesame Street."

You're starting to feel guilty for not labeling
all your family photos.

❖

You haven't blown a bubble with bubble gum for decades.

❖

When you were growing up, milk was delivered to
your house, and the milkman would give you ice chips
in the summer.

❖

You know who Sergeant Bilko was.

❖

You can't remember the last time you did the limbo.

❖

You haven't turned a somersault for at least a quarter
of a century.

❖

Your first pen came with a bottle of ink.

You had a Big Chief tablet.

❖

The screen on your family's first television set looked
like a porthole.

❖

Sometimes you refer to the refrigerator as the "icebox."

❖

You remember when a movie cost a quarter and a box of
popcorn cost a dime.

❖

You once owned a car that ran on ethyl.

❖

You can name four original Mouseketeers.

❖

You can sing jingles from TV cigarette commercials.

You know some of the verses to "Davy Crockett."

❖

You think of Michael Landon as "Little Joe."

❖

You know exactly where you were on
November 22, 1963.

❖

You remember when a typical family had one car,
one TV, one phone, and one bathroom.

❖

You remember when telephone prefixes had names like
BLackburn, ATwater, or KLondike.

❖

You remember when addresses had postal zones.

❖

You remember when dimes, quarters, and half-dollars
were really made of silver.

You remember when "banker's hours" meant 10 A.M. to 3 P.M., Monday through Friday.

❖

You remember when stores were closed on Sunday.

❖

In school you learned how to "duck and cover" to avoid nuclear annihilation.

Household items common when you were a kid are
now found in antique shops.

Stuff
· · · · · · · · ·

You have enough stuff to fill two houses.

❖

You like what comedian George Carlin had to
say about "stuff."

❖

You own only white underwear.

❖

You have a favorite pair of socks.

❖

You have a ratty bathrobe that you won't part with
because "they just don't make them like this anymore."

You no longer remember during which decade you bought your favorite slippers.

❖

You recently bought your first brand-new car.

❖

Your car is paid for.

❖

Your monthly mortgage payment is more than the total cost of your first car.

❖

You own two cars that cost more than your first house.

❖

You're not sure if you're pleased that the first car you owned is now considered a "classic."

❖

You haven't bought a new swimsuit since the Nixon administration.

You had to replace the lifetime battery in your watch.

❖

You've outlived the lifetime warranty on your car's shock absorbers.

❖

You don't bother opening mail addressed to "occupant."

❖

You once owned a baseball card that would be worth more than five thousand dollars today.

❖

You've almost forgiven your mother for throwing out your baseball card that would be worth more than five thousand dollars today.

❖

You have magazines from five years ago in your "to read" pile.

You have fifteen years' worth of old *National Geographic* magazines taking up space in your attic, garage, or basement.

❖

Household items common when you were a kid are now found in antique shops.

❖

Your favorite perfume or after-shave lotion is so outdated it's back in style.

❖

You have two complete wardrobes: one pre- and one post-diet.

❖

You buy yourself exactly what you want for Christmas.

❖

You can afford wine that comes with a cork.

The half-empty jar of instant coffee in your kitchen cupboard is so old it's turned to stone.

❖

You paid an exorbitant amount of money for a piece of furniture just like the one your grandmother threw out thirty years ago.

❖

You buy jeans advertised as having a bit more room in the seat.

❖

You won't part with your old LPs or that stack of 45s.

❖

You're beginning to realize that time is more important than things, no matter how nice those things are.

The liquor-store clerk laughs when you ask if you need
to show your ID.

All Things Considered

You're thinking of buying a cemetery plot.

❖

You consider twenty-five years ago "recently."

❖

You've decided on the title for that novel you're going to write and know who's going to play the lead when it's made into a movie.

❖

You're thinking about getting a subscription to *Modern Maturity*.

❖

You don't know the latest slang word for "good," but you're pretty sure it's not "groovy."

You've gotten used to the years going fast, but now it's the decades that are flying by.

❖

You know almost as many people who are dead as who are living.

❖

You're shocked when the clerk tells you the total cost for one small sack of groceries.

❖

The liquor-store clerk laughs when you ask if you need to show your ID.

❖

You first heard the "latest" joke that's making the rounds about twenty years ago.

❖

You don't need a calculator to multiply any numbers up to twelve times twelve.

You read *1984* when the story was "way off in the future."

❖

You still think of Beijing as Peking.

❖

You don't want pizza for dinner every night.

❖

You can easily name the last ten U.S. presidents.

❖

You preferred things the way they were and can tolerate how they are, but you don't look forward to how things will be.

❖

You think it's simply common sense to wear galoshes when it's raining.

❖

You don't really trust anyone under thirty. No, better yet, thirty-five.

You've joined a fraternal organization and don't think the
hats are funny.

Friends, Neighbors, and Former Classmates

You hang around with younger people, hoping to blend in.

❖

You hang around with older people, hoping to be referred to as "The Kid."

❖

You've joined a fraternal organization and don't think the hats are funny.

❖

People are starting to give you gifts like stationery, dusting powder, and bath oil beads.

You can't believe how much the family down the block got when they sold their itty-bitty house.

❖

You love new neighbors as long as they return their garbage cans to the backyard on the same day the trash collectors come and they don't play loud music after 9 P.M.

❖

You're considered an old-timer around the neighborhood.

❖

You've accepted the fact that your lawn will never be as green as your neighbor's, but you love it when large dogs use his yard as a bathroom.

❖

The little kids next door have asked if it's okay to call you "Grandma" or "Grandpa."

❖

You don't bicker with the neighbors, figuring they'll move or die soon enough.

You don't care what the neighbors say, you're going to keep those Christmas lights up all year long.

❖

You wake up in the middle of the night and spend hours trying to remember the name of the kid who sat behind you in freshman algebra.

❖

You no longer care that you didn't have a date for the senior prom.

❖

The thought of a chance meeting with that grade-school classmate you had a crush on still makes your heart flutter.

❖

At your class reunion, you notice two things:

1. All your classmates are middle-aged.

2. The "wild" kids have become grandparents or are now ordained.

You're jealous of high-school classmates who joined the military, served twenty or twenty-five years, and are now retiring.

❖

In your old neighborhood, the greasy burger joint at the end of the block is now an upscale sushi bar.

❖

Now when you drive by that big, fancy house on the corner of your old block, you think, "Boy, am I glad I don't have to heat or air-condition that monster."

❖

All of your new friends are middle-aged.

❖

You like being around people who remember the days when candy bars cost a nickel and the worst thing a teenager said was "damn."

❖

When you go out to dinner with friends, you calculate who owes how much down to the last penny.

When a friend you haven't seen or heard from in ten years calls, you still immediately recognize the voice.

❖

You're always extra nice to that small group of people who know your high-school nickname but have promised not to tell your spouse or kids.

You think crawling into bed with a new murder
mystery is fun.

Fun and Games

You've never beaten a video game in your life.

❖

You think all major league players are kids.

❖

You know baseball and football should be played
on real grass.

❖

The mere thought of aerobic exercise makes you sweat.

❖

You know how to do the bunny hop.

You don't bother tramping around in the rough, looking for a lost golf ball anymore.

❖

You consider nine holes of miniature golf rigorous exercise.

❖

You're willing to admit you're never going to make it into the Professional Golfers Association but have dreams of joining the senior PGA tour.

❖

Your arm gets sore watching bowling on TV.

❖

You think "60 Minutes" is entertaining as well as educational.

❖

You know there used to be more fish, and fewer fishermen, years ago.

A new rod and reel costs more than your first
boat and motor.

❖

That little bit of recreational property you had your eye
on for so many years is now part of the
supermall parking lot.

❖

You cheat at crossword puzzles and don't feel
guilty about it.

❖

Your poker group has banned smoking, and the players
drink more mineral water than beer.

❖

You look forward to bingo night.

❖

You like to shout out the answers whenever you
watch "Jeopardy!"

The only "hot" songs you can play on your old guitar, saxophone, or trombone were famous during 1962.

❖

You've noticed that you've never seen a jogger who appeared to be having a good time.

❖

You think crawling into bed with a new murder mystery is fun.

❖

You love going to all-you-can-eat buffet restaurants with dessert bars.

❖

Your idea of recreation is eating take-out Chinese food right from the carton.

❖

You think that dozing off in your recliner is fun.

You don't want to go anywhere you haven't been before.

❖

You think the highlight of Sunday morning is completing the "What's Different?" puzzle in the comics section of the newspaper.

❖

You won't admit that you've never found Waldo.

In winter, you're a firm believer in "Shovel less,
salt more."

On the Home Front

You gladly pay someone else to clean the gutters.

❖

That little apple tree you planted in the backyard
is thirty feet tall.

❖

You're ready to move into a smaller house.

❖

You would seriously consider moving into a smaller
house, but then you'd have to clean out your basement,
attic, *and* garage.

❖

You converted one of the kids' bedrooms into
a den you never use.

You find it easier to call the repair service.

❖

You decorate your house for every major holiday.

❖

You don't have any more boxes of junk at your parents' place.

❖

You have more "miscellaneous" drawers than any other kind.

❖

You always wipe your feet before you go inside.

❖

You know when to go to the hardware store and get a new washer for a leaky faucet and when to call the plumber.

Your monthly mortgage payments cover more principal than interest.

❖

The estimate for the addition to your house is more than the original cost of the entire structure.

❖

In winter, you're a firm believer in "Shovel less, salt more."

❖

Your home may not be a castle, but you feel pretty good sitting in your favorite chair, holding the remote control.

❖

You can't believe it's already time to repaint the living room.

❖

That nice house you didn't buy years ago because the monthly payments would have been one hundred dollars more, just sold for more than half a million.

Your house would be incredibly roomy if your kids had taken their stuff when they moved out.

❖

Your house would have adequate space if your kids hadn't brought so much new stuff with them when they moved back in.

❖

You've learned to live without enough closet space.

❖

There's so much junk stored under your bed, there's no room for "dust bunnies."

❖

Your old kitchen cabinets suddenly look *really* good after getting an estimate for new ones.

❖

The "new" chair in your living room is ten years old.

You'd have a garage sale, but you're too embarrassed to have your neighbors see the odd assortment of junk you've collected over the years.

❖

Your annual electric bill is more than what your parents' first home cost.

❖

You've started to read ads and articles on retirement communities.

❖

You wonder how much you could get for your house and how much a condo would cost.

Your new doctor looks like a teenager.

Health

Your new doctor looks like a teenager.

❖

You find yourself paying closer attention to TV ads for hemorrhoid ointments.

❖

You've had a lower G.I.

❖

You wonder what Geritol really does.

❖

You know there's an odorless version of Ben-Gay.

You automatically look at the "large-boned" column of any height-weight chart.

❖

You know which brand of laxative tastes best.

❖

You have a favorite antacid.

❖

You always wash your hands after going to the bathroom.

❖

You think restaurant portions are too big.

❖

You don't eat fried foods.

❖

You think about your arteries.

You realize no one is immortal.

❖

You realize you're not immortal.

❖

You know which foods give you gas.

❖

You can afford steak but prefer tuna.

❖

You had to find a new dentist because yours retired.

❖

You don't think root-canal jokes are funny.

❖

When you hear the word "bridge," you don't think "card game" or "Golden Gate."

You floss once a day.

❖

You know which breakfast cereals are low in sugar
and high in fiber.

❖

You've switched to decaffeinated tea.

❖

You find yourself thinking, "This is a good source of fiber."

❖

You've spent a lot of time dealing with nose hair.

❖

You know what your cholesterol level is.

❖

You know what "systolic" and "diastolic" mean.

You buy the jumbo-size bottle of pain relievers.

❖

You take vitamins regularly.

❖

You're on a first-name basis with your chiropractor.

❖

You like reading articles that advise people your
age not to jog.

❖

You weigh exactly the same amount as you did in high
school—until you put your other foot on the scale.

❖

You know what liposuction does.

❖

A part of you is hoping scientists will come up with a cure
for death before you seriously face it.

You once owned a coonskin cap.

The Good Old Days

You know that when it comes to hair care,
"a little dab will do ya."

❖

You think *The Catcher in the Rye* is a racy book.

❖

The leech scene from *The African Queen* still gives
you the willies.

❖

You know there will never be another dance number like
Gene Kelly's "Singin' in the Rain."

❖

Your family owned a Studebaker.

You remember how relieved your parents were when a vaccine for polio was discovered.

❖

You saw Elvis on "The Ed Sullivan Show."

❖

You attended a 3–D movie back when everyone really liked the cardboard eyeglasses they passed out in the lobby.

❖

To you, the Yankees will always mean Mickey Mantle and Roger Maris.

❖

You liked it when Ricky sang at the end of "Ozzie and Harriet."

❖

You remember when Marlon Brando was skinny.

You believed June Lockhart really could understand what
Lassie was trying to tell her.

❖

You once owned a coonskin cap.

❖

You have fond memories of your Hula Hoop.

❖

You dreamed of being a Rebel Without a Cause.

❖

You had a big crush on Annette.

❖

You can name the three kids on "Father Knows Best."

❖

You used to pledge allegiance to a flag that had
forty-eight stars.

At least one family on your old block seriously considered building a bomb shelter.

❖

You know Gilligan used to be Maynard G. Krebs.

❖

You practiced the twist in private before attempting it at the sock hop in the school gymnasium.

❖

You know Sean Connery is *the* James Bond.

❖

You used to say "far out."

❖

You thought *Jonathan Livingston Seagull* was deep.

You're absolutely shocked when you realize
Marilyn Monroe died at thirty-six, Martin Luther King, Jr.,
at thirty-nine, John F. Kennedy at forty-six, and
Judy Garland at forty-seven.

❖

You sometimes wonder how old Janis Joplin and
Jimi Hendrix would be today.

❖

You still wish the Beatles had stayed together.

❖

You can't believe the Rolling Stones are still going.

You're thinking about getting a little red sports car.

Enjoying Your Mid-Life Crisis

....

You're thinking about getting a little red sports car.

❖

You've joined a support group.

❖

You've come to realize the family you grew up
in was dysfunctional.

❖

You've come to realize your immediate family
is dysfunctional.

❖

You've come to realize there's no such thing as a
functional family.

You wonder if you should have gotten an
advanced degree.

❖

You wonder if you should have dropped out of graduate
school and pursued that singing career.

❖

You want to open a bookstore.

❖

You want to own a restaurant.

❖

You want to go back to school.

❖

You want to be a painter, playwright, sculptor,
or relief pitcher.

❖

You think about all the things that start to go wrong
with a car once it hits fifty thousand miles.

You can accept that you're never going to drive around the country in an old, beat-up VW bus or spend a summer bumming around Europe.

❖

You're not sure what you want to do with the rest of your life, but you're pretty sure you don't want to keep on doing what you've already done.

❖

You'd like to shake the hand of the person who first said that youth is wasted on the young.

❖

You like the idea that you can do something really stupid and blame it on your mid-life crisis.

When you stare up at fluffy clouds, you no longer see baby lambs and bunny rabbits, but rolls of flab and crowded tombstones.

It's All in Your Mind

You make lists so you won't forget things, and then you misplace the lists.

❖

You know the beginnings and the punch lines of several great jokes, but the middle parts are all a little hazy.

❖

You enter a room to get something and can't for the life of you remember what it was.

❖

You've memorized the recipe for Nestlé's Original Toll House cookies.

❖

You constantly call your kids by their siblings' names.

You can recite most of the preamble to the Constitution.

❖

You know it's foolish to enter a grocery store without a shopping list.

❖

You remember the family's phone number from when you were a kid.

❖

You have a "master" calendar and several smaller ones.

❖

You automatically wake up early on weekends and can't fall back asleep.

❖

Your mind runs through the four basic food groups and the nutritional pyramid as you sink your teeth into a slice of thick-crust pepperoni pizza with extra cheese.

You wish you had more time to think.

❖

When you stare up at fluffy clouds, you no longer see baby lambs and bunny rabbits, but rolls of flab and crowded tombstones.

❖

You know mental health is often more fragile than physical health.

❖

You've become a master at coming up with excuses.

❖

You can name only five of the seven dwarfs—four if you're willing to admit there isn't a "Sleazy."

❖

If you hear certain children's songs, they will rattle around in your head for days.

You've decided you don't want to know what's going on in the typical teenager's mind.

❖

You wonder when your parents became so calm and philosophical.

❖

You can't remember more than two lines from "Trees" by Joyce Kilmer or "Gunga Din" by Rudyard Kipling, but you've never forgotten a single word of the limericks that begin "There was a young lady from Venus. . . ."

❖

You know the numbers for a combination padlock that you lost twenty years ago.

❖

You're trying to figure out if some older people don't complain because they're happy most of the time, or are happy most of the time because they don't complain.

❖

You're hoping for a really good epitaph.

You know that taking time to smell the roses sometimes means getting a little fertilizer on your shoes.

❖

You know that many things in life are a case of mind over matter: If you don't mind, they don't matter.

❖

You've noticed that people in their twenties think you're old and people in their seventies think you're young.

❖

You realize you're not quite old enough to get away with being eccentric, but you're making plans for the day you are.

By the time the last candle on your birthday cake is lit,
the first one is almost completely melted.

Happy Birthday to You

By the time the last candle on your birthday cake is lit, the first one is almost completely melted.

❖

You can't blow out all the candles on your cake.

❖

Your family saved money by buying your birthday candles in bulk.

❖

You vehemently deny this is the birthday you hit middle age.

❖

You're willing to admit that in a few years you *might* be approaching middle age.

An item just like the one you received for your fifth birthday is now on display in the Smithsonian.

❖

At least half of the famous people listed in the newspaper who share your birthday are younger than you.

❖

You celebrate the day of your birth, not the year.

❖

Your younger siblings never tire of throwing surprise birthday parties for you.

❖

You tell others your age has peaked and that you've started counting your birthdays backward.

❖

You prefer the phrase "thirty-nine plus."

❖

You remember the day your dad turned this age and now marvel at how young he was.

You're proud to take advantage of the free-meal-on-your-birthday offer at Denny's.

❖

When the waiters and waitresses bring out a small complimentary dessert and gather to belt out "Happy Birthday," you shut them up by saying, "Sing one note, and you can kiss your tip good-bye."

❖

You stand next to your wrinkly great-aunt when all the photos are taken.

❖

It feels like you celebrated your last birthday about a week ago.

❖

You know that being "middle-aged" isn't really so bad, and you've started making the distinction between "*young* old" people and "*old* old" people.

❖

You realize it's too late for you to die young or to leave a good-looking corpse.

Order Form

Qty.	Title	Author	Order No.	Unit Cost	Total
	Are You Over the Hill?	Dodds, B.	4265	$6.00	
	Best Baby Shower Book	Cooke, C.	1239	$7.00	
	Best Party Book	Warner, P.	6089	$7.00	
	Best Wedding Shower Book	Cooke, C.	6059	$7.00	
	Dads Say the Dumbest Things!	Lansky/Jones	4220	$6.00	
	David, We're Pregnant!	Johnston, L.	1049	$6.00	
	Do They Ever Grow Up?	Johnston, L.	1089	$6.00	
	Grandma Knows Best	McBride, M.	4009	$6.00	
	Hi, Mom! Hi, Dad!	Johnston, L.	1139	$6.00	
	How to Embarrass Your Kids	Holleman/Sherins	4005	$6.00	
	How to Outsmart Your Kids	Dodds, B.	4190	$6.00	
	How to Survive 40th Birthday	Dodds, B.	4260	$6.00	
	Italian Without Words	Cangelosi/Carpini	5100	$5.00	
	Kids Pick the Funniest Poems	Lansky, B.	2410	$14.00	
	Moms Say the Funniest Things!	Lansky, B.	4280	$6.00	
	Mother Murphy's Law	Lansky, B.	1149	$4.50	
	Mother Murphy's 2nd Law	Lansky, B.	4010	$4.50	
	New Adventures of Mother Goose	Lansky, B.	2420	$15.00	
	What's So Funny About Getting Old?	Noland, J.	4205	$6.00	
	Wierd Wonders	Schreiber, B.	4120	$4.95	
	World's Funniest Roast Jokes	Stangland, R.	4030	$6.00	
				Subtotal	
		Shipping and Handling (see below)			
		MN residents add 6.5% sales tax			
				Total	

YES! Please send me the books indicated above. Add $2.00 shipping and handling for the first book and 50¢ for each additional book. Add $2.50 to total for books shipped to Canada. Overseas postage will be billed. Allow up to 4 weeks for delivery. Send check or money order payable to Meadowbrook Press. No cash or C.O.D.'s, please. Prices subject to change without notice. **Quantity discounts available upon request.**

Send book(s) to:

Name _____ Address _____

City _____ State _____ Zip _____

Telephone (_____)_____ P.O. number (if necessary) _____

Payment via: ❏ Check or money order payable to Meadowbrook Press
(No cash or C.O.D.'s, please) Amount enclosed $ _____
❏ Visa (for orders over $10.00 only.) ❏ MasterCard (for orders over $10.00 only.)

Account # _____ Signature _____ Exp. Date _____

A **FREE** Meadowbrook Press catalog is available upon request.
You can also phone us for orders of $10.00 or more at 1-800-338-2232.

Mail to: Meadowbrook, Inc.
18318 Minnetonka Boulevard, Deephaven, MN 55391
(612) 473-5400   Toll-Free 1-800-338-2232   Fax (612) 475-0736